Yoga and Kāma

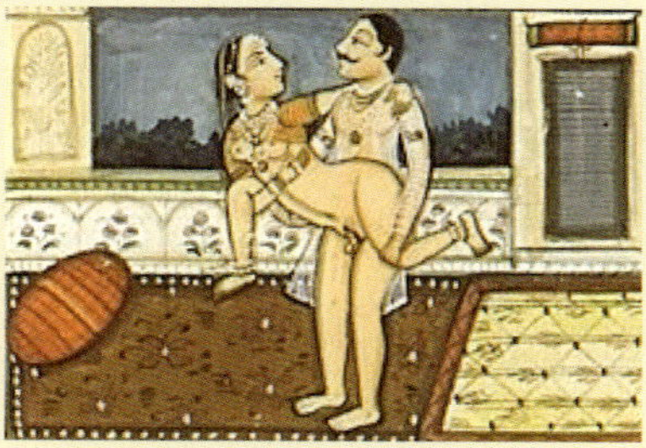

Yoga and Kāma

~The Acrobatics of Love~

Alka Pande

SPEAKING TIGER

SPEAKING TIGER BOOKS LLP
125A, Ground Floor, Shahpur Jat, near Asiad Village,
New Delhi 110049

First published by Speaking Tiger Books 2022

ISBN: 978-93-5447-231-2

10 9 8 7 6 5 4 3 2 1

Typeset in Cormorant Garamond by SÜRYA, New Delhi
Printed at : SBM Industries Pvt Ltd, Rai (www.sbmprints.com)

Above: Man with a woman in the camel pose. Carving from a wooden chariot, Tamil Nadu, 19th century. Collection of Beroze and Michel Sabatier, La Rochelle.

Page 1: Image from a poster depicting 84 asanas for love-making, inspired by the *Kamasutra*. Nathdwara School, 19th century.

One of the 92 asanas from an illustrated edition of the *Ratirahasya* ('Secrets of Love') by Koka, more popularly known as the *Kokashahstra*. Jaipur School, late 19th century. Private collection.

~ Introduction ~

Yujyate anena iti yogaha
(That which joins is yoga.)

Shiva, the great God, has infinite attributes; in him all aspects of life, often contradictory, are subsumed and reach their perfection. Everything is sacred, nothing is profane. He is the ultimate Yogi (celibate ascetic) and he is also the ultimate Bhogi (master of pleasure). In the shastras it is said that Shiva is Lord of Yoga—Aadi Yogi—and he first imparted his knowledge of yoga to Parvati on the night of their union after they married. It was then that they began their cosmic dance of love, and it is in this context that these words were spoken: *Yujyate anena iti yogaha.*

In India today, yoga and kama are not mentioned in the same breath, because the former is thought to be about spirituality and asceticism and the latter about psychological and physical pleasure, and never the twain shall meet. This false dichotomy is the unfortunate result of a twisted Indian modernity which has internalized—and indeed, made holy—the terrible Victorian prudery that was imposed in the colonial era on the remarkably liberal and life-affirming ideas of Hinduism. Ideas that were also at the heart of Bhakti and Sufi mysticism, in which the yearning for union with God is expressed in the language of pure eroticism.

Lord Ṣhiva is Aadi Purusha—Ishwara, the Supreme Consciousness—before he is Aadi Yogi, or indeed any of his various forms. And as Aadi Purusha—or just Purusha—he describes 112 ways to enter into the ultimate, transcendental state of consciousness. These include breath awareness and control, concentration on various centres (chakras) in the body, non-dual awareness, chanting the primal sound, training of the body in balance and mindfulness through intricate postures, and contemplation through each of the senses. Shiva is believed to have taught Parvati, his first and ideal student, all of this through 84 asanas of yoga (of which only a very few could be apprehended by mortals, and just about five are described in the classical texts). But if Shiva is Purusha, the embodiment of supreme consciousness, Parvati is not merely his student; she is Aadi Shakti, or Prakriti, the embodiment of supreme knowledge—which is consciousness in action. Without her, there would be no creation. All that exists in the universe—in fact, the universe itself—results from the union of Purusha and Prakriti. In other words, it results from from kama. And kama began with yoga.

~

Yoga, which is equally about the mind, the body and the soul, is the science of ultimate balance—between dharma (duty, or 'right living'), artha (economic well-being), kama (erotic desire) and moksha (enlightenment or liberation), which are the four goals of life in classical Hinduism. Sexual satisfaction is thus essential for a full and healthy experience of life. The most visible manifestations of yoga are physical poses or asanas and these were the easiest to depict. Hence the profusion in India's pre-modern sculpture and art of people engaged in a variety of sexual acts, the positions inspired directly by yoga asanas.

Sometimes, especially in miniatures produced from

the 16th or 17th century CE onwards, these positions seem utterly improbable and beyond the capacity of any human being. These over-the-top acrobatics are not to be taken literally; they are about uninhibited play and delight. But their root also lies in the same philosophy of celebration and a balanced, pragmatic life that is the essence of yoga.

Scholars and aesthetes have offered other explanations for the fevered, exaggerated and improbable love-making that is seen on the outer walls of many Hindu temples and in folk paintings and artefacts which were sold near temples (in some places they still are—the pattachitra scrolls in Puri, for instance). One theory is that all the images of sexual excess overwhelm and then cleanse the senses as we approach the inner shrine and the sanctum sanctorum; our minds and hearts are sated and purged of desire, and thus fertile soil for divine grace.

Another theory, which would apply more to miniatures and similar erotic art, is that the fevered sexuality might have been caused by the strain on sexual freedom in medieval India—thus, sex, condemned in real life, came to be celebrated wildly in art.

Either way—disciplined and intricate yogic poses, or eye-popping contortions and acrobatics—the aim is to wholeheartedly accept a great gift of life and immerse one's senses in erotic bliss. Just as one must also immerse oneself in worldly knowledge at the appropriate time, and then in spiritual and transcendental knowledge.

~

Both kama and yoga are central to the *Kamasutra*, the mother of all the *kama shastras* (erotic texts) of India. The Western world, and even many Indians—including those who are ashamed of our traditions of erotica and also those who are not—view the *Kamasutra* as only a book about sexual gymnastics, aphrodisiacs, love bites and so on. It is in fact a remarkable guide to pleasurable living, aesthetics, grooming, patience in indulgence, and sexual etiquette.

One of the first Indian sages to reflect on kama was Shvetaketu, son of Uddalaka, who recorded a summary of the sacred bull Nandi's descriptions of Shiva and Parvati's coupling. Nandi, Shiva's vahana (vehicle) and doorkeeper, is believed to have witnessed the epic love rituals of his master and mistress and in stunned enlightenment, he later whispered them to Shvetaketu. Over centuries, other sages—Swayambhu, Manu, Brihaspati and others—interpreted and expanded Nandi's and Shvetaketu's revelations. Until finally, sometime in the 3rd century CE, a celibate yogi, Vatsyayana, refined and collated all their work to produce the *Kamasutra*. There are also versions of this myth which say that Nandi revealed the secrets of divine love-making directly to Vatsyayana.

The *Kamasutra* became the iconic book for a pleasurable life to be led by men and women. In pre-modern India, the study of the erotic was an extremely significant and substantial part of Indian philosophy and literature. Vatsyayana's masterpiece inspired several Sanskrit scholars, poets and writers who established a distinct genre of writing which came to be known as the *Kama shastra*.

The *Kamasutra* was also a defining influence on pre-modern sculpture and art. And in the evolved spirit of living that came from liberal Hinduism, the *Kamasutra* and other *kama shastras* inspired art in the service of the divine. We see this in the exquisite erotic sculptures on the walls of the temples in Khajuraho, Konarak, Hampi and Modhera, among other sites, where men and women are shown in states of *mithuna* (intimacy) and *maithuna* (sexual acts). In the advait or non-dual philosophy of Hinduism, this is the union of atma (soul) with paramatma (God) expressed in the metaphor of sexual union. Therefore, nothing is prohibited, nothing is sullied by shame, and we see remarkable depictions of frankly sexual yogic poses and acrobatics.

Devangana Desai writes in her book *Erotic Sculpture of India*: 'In sculptural art, there are some postures which do involve Hatha Yoga techniques. These are seen in the head down poses of Khajuraho, Padhavli, Belur...Hatha yogic techniques can also be seen in some of the intricate sitting and sleeping poses of Bhubaneswar, Lingaraja and Konarak.' Alex Comfort, writing on India's *kama shastras*, observes: 'One complete sequence of *bandhas* from Vatsyayana on appears to derive directly from yogic exercises, and this sequence becomes longer and more complicated in the latter erotic treaties, until it includes really exorbitant tours de force, such as coition with the woman head down in sirshasana.'

Evidence of 'sexo-yogic' positions is also found in Tantric Buddhist traditions. One such is Tantric Sadhana for the immobilization of the three jewels, i.e., thought, breath and semen. The Yab-Yum image of Tantric Buddhism is symbolic of delayed ejaculation or coitus reservatus for the purpose of heightened consciousness.

The interesting point to note is that it is usually the women—slim, svelte and athletic—and not the men, who are shown in intricate yogic asanas. Probably they were the facilitators for *kayasadhana* (body discipline). Or they were courtesans whom male patrons turned to for help when their libido was flagging.

~

Many yoga asanas are named after animals, for animals are flexible and agile by nature, or they perish. The ancient Indian sages observed the flora and fauna of their ecosystem closely and realized that imitation of certain animal postures and forms led to the energizing of human hormones. Not surprisingly, in sculpture and paintings inspired by the *Kamasutra* and other erotic texts, couples and groups having sex are shown in asanas that are directly connected to certain animals and are named after them.

These representations are found across the subcontinent, whether on grand edifices or in humble artworks. A 19th century wooden chariot from Tamil Nadu has the most beautiful carving of a man and a woman engaged in *maithuna*, with the woman bending backwards in the Ustrasana or camel pose. A draft drawing on yellowing paper from Rajasthan shows the breathtaking, fluid grace of the crocodile pose, with the man and woman arching into and away from each other. A chatai, or reed mat, that a friend once slept on during her stay in an Andhra village had charming woven images of couples joined in the mrigasana or deer pose...

And then there are, of course, other asanas that anyone, anywhere in the world with even the most rudimentary idea of yoga would recognize: sirshasana, the headstand, and padmasana, the lotus posture. The former is fabulously carved on the walls of the Khajuraho temples, and the latter appears in full glory in tantric art. These 'sexo-yogic' images appear again and again in sites and on surfaces where the erotic and the sacred co-exist. Spiritual and erotic bliss emerge from the same source. It is only natural, then, that yoga and kama have been so intimately connected.

Enjoy the images in the pages that follow—you will be awestruck, excited, amused, astounded and educated.

ALKA PANDE
Vasant, 2022

Painting from an illuminated *kama shastra* text in Persian translation. Probably 19th century.

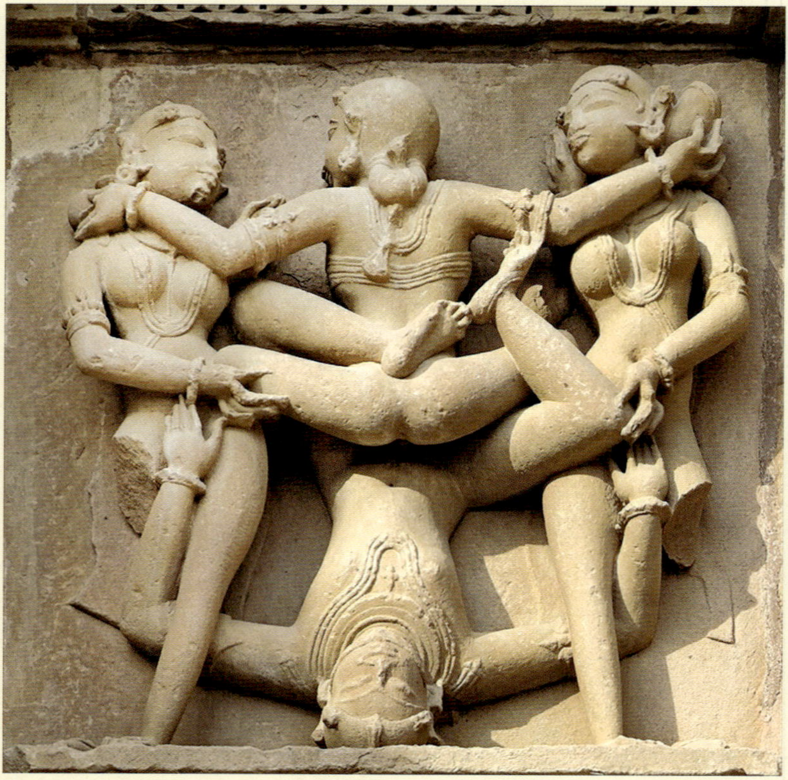

Perhaps the most famous sculpture from the Khajuraho group of temples. This one adorns a wall of the 11th century CE Kandariya Mahadeva temple.

Also from Khajuraho—a sculpture on the exterior wall of the 10th century Lakshmana Temple.

Above: Lovers Embracing. Folio from a private album of erotica. Bhaktapur, Nepal, 1675 CE. Los Angeles County Museum of Art (LACMA).

Opposite: Nayika with a pankha to fan the flames of passion. Jodhpur School, 19th century. Private collection.

Attendant watches in wonder. Jodhpur School, 19th century.
Private collection.

Trapeze artists. Maharashtra, 19th century. Collection of Beroze and Michel Sabatier, La Rochelle.

Perfectly matched. Sirohi School, early 19th century.
Private collection.

Lovers in flight. Sirohi School, early 19th century.
Private collection.

The skilled groomer. Jodhpur School, 19th century.
Private collection.

The skilled archer. Sirohi School, 19th century. Private collection.

Above and opposite: Folios from an 18th century illustrated adaptation of the *Kamasutra* featuring a Nepali king and a kumari. Philadelphia Museum of Art.

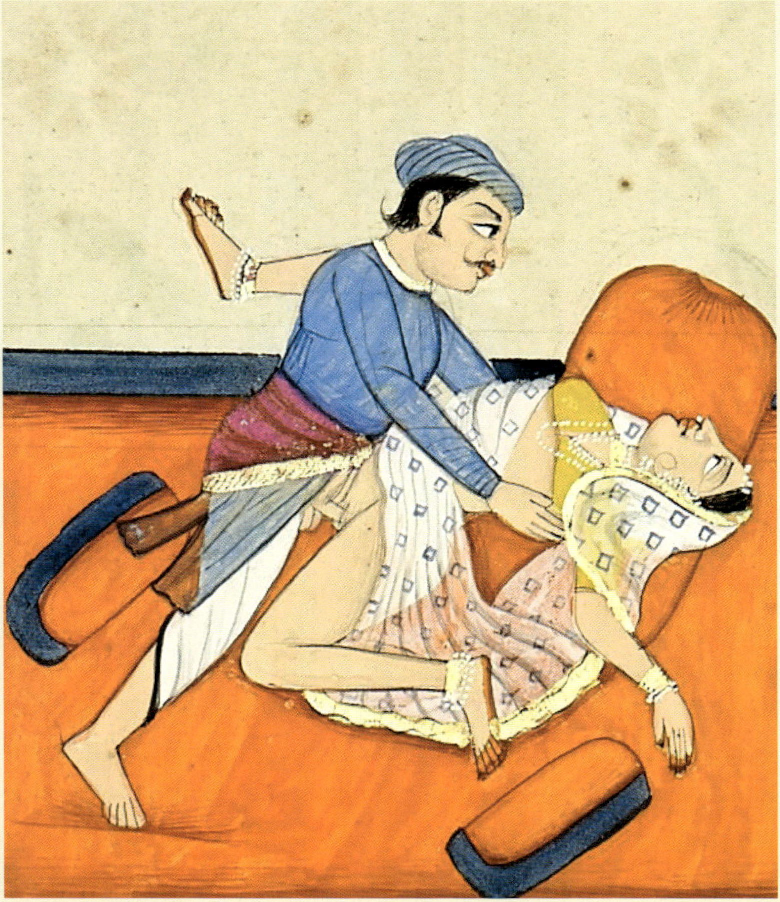

Opposite and above: Frenzy and climax. Paintings from an illustrated version of the *Kokashahstra*. Jaipur School, late 19th century. Private collection.

Above and opposite: Youth and experience; odes to sex and yoga.

Both paintings executed in the Nathdwara style in the late 19th century or early 20th. Private collection.

Above: In the throes of passion amidst nature. Rajasthan, 20th century. Collection of Beroze and Michel Sabatier, La Rochelle.

Opposite: A rugged prince and his supple lover. Jaipur school, app. 1880. Private collection.

8

Above: A lady of astonishing grace rides her man. A 19th century imitation of a Kangra School miniature of the 17th century.

Opposite page: Raja Mahendra Pal of Basholi with a favourite Rani. 1805. Cleveland Museum of Art.

The wheel of love. Painting on ivory, early 20th century. Museum of Erotics and Mythology, Brussels.

Another wheel of love. Rajasthan, beginning of the 20th century. Museum of Erotics and Mythology, Brussels.

Yoga in the service of cunnilingus and fellatio ('auparishtika' in the *Kamasutra*).

Above left: Heterosexual 69. Stone carving from the facade of a temple. Orissa, 13th century. Collection of Beroze and Michel Sabatier, La Rochelle. *Above right:* Male homosexual 69. From an early 20th century illustrated adaptation of a *kama shastra* text.

Opposite page: Woman pleases her lover as he prepares (we should hope) to return the favour. A popular drawing of uncertain provenance that has become popular on the Internet.

Embrace for the erotic kiss. From a series of paintings depicting positions for sexual intercourse. Kota School, app. 1725 CE. Walters Art Museum.

The Bodhisattva and his consort in the padmasana embrace. Detail from an erotic text of Nepal. Date unknown.

Parasparasana (literally, mutual, or face-to-face, asana). Painting from an illustrated edition of the *Ratirahasya* ('Secrets of Love') by Koka, more popularly known as the *Kokashahstra*, describing 92 asanas for sex. Jaipur School, late 19th century. Private collection.

All paintings from pages 44 to 65 are from this 19th century book.

Asana with a long and intriguing name: Streepopatasana. In which the woman is a parrot.

Baanasana, the bow asana.

Asana to quench the fire of lust.

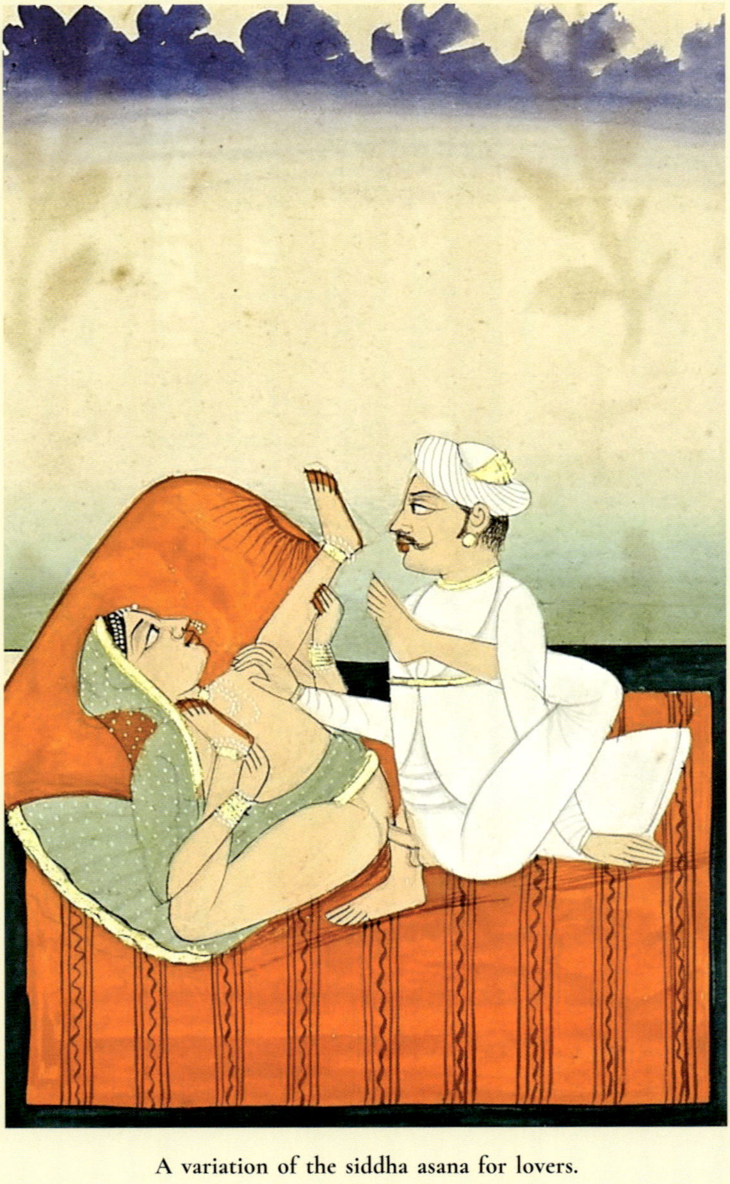

A variation of the siddha asana for lovers.

The blissful embrace asana.

Asana of perfect balance.

The asana of churning.

The scary asana.

The male asana.

The deer asana.

The asana of unbridled passion.

Asana of the patient ones.

Compact asana for intercourse in narrow spaces.

Asana inspired by the demon-slaying goddess.

Asana of the nimble one.

Opposite: Asana of the equally matched.

Above: Asana of the doubly-armed huntress.

The 'stamping love' asana.

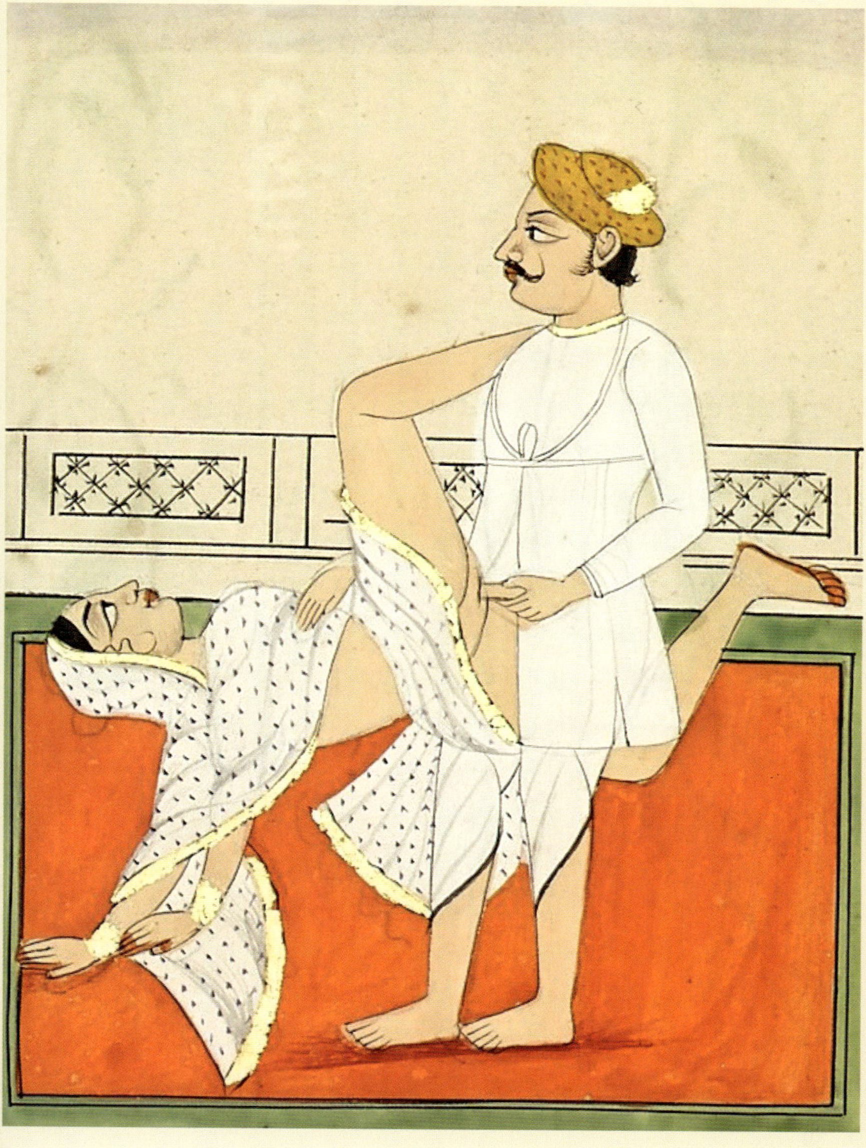

Called the adharachanha asana, this athletic asana is open to interpretation.

The blooming lotus asana.

Asana inspired by the dancing peacock.

Woman sitting on a man and two pillows. Sketch on paper, Company Style, 19th century. Collection of Beroze and Michel Sabatier, La Rochelle.

The king with the young queen in an extreme variation of the makarasana. Draft drawing from the Jaipur School, 19th century. Private Collection.

Above: The veena player. Tamil Nadu, 19th century. Collection of Beroze and Michel Sabatier, La Rochelle.

Opposite page: Beautiful gymnast and her royal supplicant.

Alka Pande trained as an art historian and has written prolifically on Indology and Art History. She is the author of several books with a special interest in gender and sexuality; her PhD thesis was on the theme of Ardhanarishvara. She has written extensively on erotic Indian literature and art as well. Her books include *Masterpieces of Indian Art*; *Shringara: The Many Faces of Indian Beauty*; *Body Sutra: Tracing the Human Form Through Art & Imagination*; *The New Age Kamasutra for Women* and *Pha(bu)llus: A Cultural History*.

Alka Pande was awarded the Chevalier dans l'Ordre des Arts et des Lettres in 2006 by the French government.